Meditations

ROGER EPP
ONLY LEAVE
A TRACE

RHONDA HARDER EPP, Illustrator

The University of Alberta Press

Published by

The University of Alberta Press
Ring House 2
Edmonton, Alberta, Canada T6G 2E1
www.uap.ualberta.ca

Copyright © 2017 Roger Epp
Illustrations Copyright © 2017 Rhonda Harder Epp

LIBRARY AND ARCHIVES CANADA
CATALOGUING IN PUBLICATION

Epp, Roger, 1958–, author
    Only leave a trace : meditations / Roger Epp ; Rhonda Harder Epp, illustrator.

Issued in print and electronic formats.
ISBN 978-1-77212-266-4 (softcover).—
ISBN 978-1-77212-312-8 (EPUB).—
ISBN 978-1-77212-313-5 (Kindle).—
ISBN 978-1-77212-314-2 (PDF)

    1. Educational leadership. 2. School management and organization. I. Title.

LB2805.E67 2017   371.2   C2016-908088-9
                            C2016-908089-7

First edition, first printing, 2017.
First printed and bound in Canada by Friesens, Altona, Manitoba.
Copyediting and proofreading by Maya Fowler-Sutherland.

All rights reserved. No part of this publication may be reproduced, stored in a retrieval system, or transmitted in any form or by any means (electronic, mechanical, photocopying, recording, or otherwise) without prior written consent. Contact the University of Alberta Press for further details.

The University of Alberta Press supports copyright. Copyright fuels creativity, encourages diverse voices, promotes free speech, and creates a vibrant culture. Thank you for buying an authorized edition of this book and for complying with the copyright laws by not reproducing, scanning, or distributing any part of it in any form without permission. You are supporting writers and allowing University of Alberta Press to continue to publish books for every reader.

The University of Alberta Press gratefully acknowledges the support received for its publishing program from the Government of Canada, the Canada Council for the Arts, and the Government of Alberta through the Alberta Media Fund.

I am become a puzzle to myself.
 —AUGUSTINE, *The Confessions*, Book X

His ceremonies laid by, in his nakedness he is but a man.
 —SHAKESPEARE, *Henry V*, 4.1

Yet who among us has never, from time to time, been forced into playing some role? The important thing is to be conscious of that role and to be able to reflect upon it and one's relation to it.
 —VÁCLAV HAVEL, *To the Castle and Back*

To dwell means to leave traces.
 —WALTER BENJAMIN, *The Writer of Modern Life*

Contents

ix *Preface*

Set on a Wall 1
3 Only Leave a Trace
4 Hard Times
6 The Teacher of Machiavelli
7 *Vikingskipshuset*, Oslo
8 Make Yourself Big

Under
11 If Students Ask
12 Reciprocity
13 Easter Weekend
14 Years of Promises to See this Day
15 Round Dance
16 Dog Sled
17 Those Who Build Bridges
18 While Stephen Lewis Sleeps

Over
21 Highway Time
22 A Life as Thin as Paper
23 Straw-Men and Politicians
24 Six Years, No Accidents
25 A Curator of Tears
26 Another Year, And No Disaster
27 Job Description
29 This is the Way the World Will End or, How a Dean Thinks

Around 1

33 Someplace, Not No-Place

34 Saturday Morning at the Co-op

36 Doctor Fowler

37 Reading University

38 Boundaries

39 First Things, And How Wine Was Served on Campus

41 Resource Curse

Around 2

45 On Sunday They Will Walk

47 Leave a Message at the Tone

48 The Under-Painting

49 A Wednesday Night in Daysland

50 Generation Gap

51 Brainstorm

52 Return to Aberystwyth

53 Turning 50

Through

57 SE 09 31 06

Set on a Wall 2

65 Numbering the Days

66 The Old Man in Winter

68 Iron Cage

69 The Image of a Hundred Years

70 Reminders

71 Last Night in June

73 *Notes*

77 *Acknowledgements*

Preface

THIS BOOK OF MEDITATIONS is an unconventional artifact of my time as founding dean and head of the University of Alberta's Augustana Campus. The remarkable series of small miracles—mostly right people, right timing—that brought Augustana inside the province's flagship public university on July 1, 2004, as a distinctively undergraduate, liberal arts campus, in the small city of Camrose, and then the challenge of making that merger work, set in motion an intense transition period shaped by new financial resources, constant cultural translations, and, inevitably, sudden anxieties for the future over local integrity within a much bigger institution. There were no templates for this work, and no guarantees that it would be successful, as I think, on balance, it has been. While I have my own visceral memories of the long struggles—financial and otherwise—that preceded the merger, having taught at Augustana since 1990, and while I was interim vice-president (academic) in the year in which it was negotiated, these meditations are meant neither as memoir nor as front-row history of that period. They have no documentary ambitions. They do not dwell on the transition period. They do not pretend, moreover, to distill new insights either for higher education or for leadership generally in times of change—the kind that fills the shelves of airport bookshops. Instead they are short meditations on a dean's life.

These meditations take their literary inspiration from the form of the prose poem, which, as I learned from the writer Holly Iglesias, trades in "fugitive content," that is, in things that will not or cannot be said in other ways. Though these meditations reflect the rare wonder, the risk, of having done a new thing together with many others, they record only select experiences. They do so with minimal annotation. They recognize beginnings and endings, but otherwise are arranged not so much in linear time as by rough concentric circles, larger and smaller: students, office, community, family, a geographic retreat. Many of them come from the interior life or, rather, from the relentless negotiation between the personal and the public requirements of the role, to speak, intervene, judge, and act. Outside of that, they are sparingly particular. They tell only what is theirs to tell.

In a certain sense these meditations bear a resemblance to what once were called work poems, though they are written not from the shop floor, the lumber mill or the oil patch, but from the dean's office. As such, they may lack the natural advantages that accrue to a muscular, proletarian voice and the reversal of reliable caricatures—as if the distance from pallets of 2x4s or wildcat wells to verse is inherently so much longer and more exotic. These meditations share the same ambition, though, to humanize and scrutinize and uphold the integrity of an unfamiliar world of work. Their subject will be familiar enough to others who have worked in senior leadership positions in higher education settings. The choice to set them in the third person seemed most appropriate to the recollection of having played a role, however defining it might have been, for a finite period of years.

The paintings reproduced in these pages are by Rhonda Harder Epp, a visual artist and my life partner for more than three decades. They were painted at roughly the same time as many of these pieces were written. In the original, they are 5" x 5" and 5" x 7" studies created in preparation for larger canvases. Some of them appear as modernist, colour-field paintings—a radical departure in her case—but their purpose is more conceptual and unfinished. The paintings are visual meditations on the subject of walls, on what they limit, obscure and separate, but also, at least as I saw them initially, on the small creative openings that appear around those same walls, through them, under and over them. As the memory of my deanship slowly has settled, and as Rhonda moved on to windows, ladders and picket fences, I have come to wonder whether the instinct to look for the openings and therefore to imagine walls mostly as obstacles is not just an occupational requirement of university administrators in complex times, which it surely is, but an impatient narrowing of the field of vision. These paintings, in turn, now seem to me to be as much about the complexity of the walls themselves as they are about the openings. In the meditations, there are walls to knock down and get past. There are walls that demarcate spaces and difficult crossings: above all, to what is commonly and only half-jokingly called the "dark side" of university administration. But there are also walls to build and times to build them. There are walls to scale, to straddle, to reinforce. There are walls behind which to withdraw. There are walls on which to make a mark, and walls on which to lean, to rest.

SET ON A WALL 1

Only Leave a Trace

The poet is no stranger to the dean.

Here is what one knows and the other must learn: there are no innocent words; in print and in performance, precision matters; small numbers of readers, in the end, will make their own meanings mostly from the spaces left between the lines.

Here is what the poet knows: no human experience, not the best, the hardest, the loneliest, should go unwritten.

Here is the risk on which the dean, looking back, has settled: only poetry, with its peculiar discipline, can write the best, the hardest, the loneliest years of a working life without need to set the record straight or name names or settle scores or turn maudlin.

Only leave a trace. Lighten.

Hard Times

In the final year of troubles he had ceased to keep a journal. He could not write resentments anymore. He could not tell the story's end. So he kept no track of days. The cyclic consolations of the psalmist, he trusted no more than he would a slip of paper fortune: *All your hard work will soon pay off. May those who sow in tears reap with shouts of joy.* Though both messages he did not forget.

He was bullied in a meeting where the numbers were against him. The details, he kept to himself.

He heard echoes of a former war in Southeast Asia: only brutal cuts would save this college.

He took refuge in the classroom.

He met a member of the Board away from campus. For this, he knew, he could be fired.

He wrote letters for his colleagues. For himself, he sent inquiries, urgent, unashamed in search of work, but they raised no prospect, nothing here, or here. Only sympathy. Academics everywhere know for certain things are always getting worse, but how could they imagine this?

He took refuge in the classroom.

He thought hard about a buy-out in the week before the deadline, help the place, no, help himself, though what else would he do? He pitched instead a ten-point plan: the first, no layoffs. He saw a way, he thought, at least a way of buying time.

He kept his passport current in case the school in South Dakota called.

He said goodbye to Tom: he'd be crazy not to take that job. He said goodbye to students for the summer.

He found a Stephen Foster songbook for two nickels at a garage sale. *Many days you have lingered.* He was asked to come to meetings. Back and forth he shuttled, to meetings, to his daughter at the piano, where they played at harmonies: *Hard times, come again no more.* He was ready on a Monday with a motion, moved and seconded.

In June he asked all staff to stand, together, while a floor-vote decided their future. They stood. He said no to South Dakota. He had work to do.

In July he moved into the corner office, the one they called panopticon. In small steps he moved away from colleagues.

He bought new clothes. He took no holidays. He buried his resentments. He put himself in between. He thought he knew the risks.

In the final days of August, before students returned, he gave his first address. He named those who had gone and spoke words of wonder that those who were left, having endured so much, should have reconvened in a place that was both familiar and new.

The Teacher of Machiavelli

The teacher of Machiavelli tells his faculty that there is nothing more perilous, less certain of success, than to introduce a new order of things. The rest of the lesson goes without saying: that even supporters of the new will be lukewarm, skittish, prone to nostalgia until its advantages are demonstrated over time. That's just human. But he has a job to do.

The teacher of Machiavelli, erudite and worldly-wise, has read that it is best for the prince to commit his cruelties all at once, safer to be feared than loved, virtuous to adapt to circumstances before they overwhelm him. That people are always impressed by results. That most of them can judge only by appearances. So it is good to appear merciful, pious and kind—and also to know when not to be.

The teacher of Machiavelli has read that the prince should never be afraid of his own shadow.

But in sleep, night after night, he finds himself stranded on a steel beam, a tree limb, a timber plank, with a long way to fall. The dreams are no mystery. Nothing is more perilous, less certain of success. The fears he can say, he names for his faculty: that he will let them down or be crushed between old and new. He does not know if such disclosure is weakness or *virtú* or some better instinct altogether, or if anyone besides him will remember what he has said.

Vikingskipshuset, Oslo

If you unearthed a ship encased a thousand years beneath a farmer's field you could bury it again, and let it rot. Leave the dead be.

Or, painstakingly, you could disassemble it, number all the pieces, the wooden planks and iron fasteners, fabricate replacements that you cannot do without, put the ship back together in the shelter of a warehouse; then move it on a flatbed car, without jostling, people watching, wait and see, through the streets of downtown Oslo, taking up each length of track, laying it in front, just that far ahead, in the direction of the harbour barge and, at last, the museum built for it.

There is a lesson here in Norway: the recognition and care and moving of a great prize.

Make Yourself Big

Make yourself big when you enter a room, when you meet a bear in the woods. Make yourself big. Meet the eyes.

So long as you can tell what kind of bear it is, what kind of room.

UNDER

If Students Ask

If students ask, and the cause is right, he will let them bring a goat into his office and feed apples to a horse penned in the quad. He will let them sell his face on a T-shirt and plant a garden in the corner of the campus. He will shoot free-throws and sing "Danny Boy" in front of audiences. He will buy a dancing Chinese lion, with a paintbrush give it life. He will model thrift-store clothes. He will make a postcard painting on Masonite. He will ride a bus to a funeral. He will sit with students in the cafeteria and visit their *casa* in Cuba. He will write their letters of reference. He will search for words to describe all that students know that won't fit in the small boxes of a transcript.

When he was in their place he expected less. He did not know the names of presidents and deans.

But he has learned how little of learning is intelligence alone, how much is risk, friendship, trust, belonging, spaces to gather.

He grows attached to every class. At convocation, families present, he says they fill him with hope. Honestly. If students ask, he is good for one last hug.

Reciprocity

When the border closes to Canadian beef, the university in farm country has no idea, just a hunch, how many students pay their tuition with cow-calf money, how many won't be back in the fall. When the bursary is advertised—careful: rural people don't like the sound of charity or begging—the blue binder fills with home-truths, economies, honour and distress, the value of an education.

There is the student who has sold her champion show-horse and cannot ask her parents to make more sacrifices. And another: *With a struggling farm, my parents are not able to help me out. They work really hard to just support themselves. BSE has forced our lives to change completely.* This from a mother, sent by fax machine: *We are very proud of our daughter and her academic accomplishments. We are trying to make it possible.* The surprise of the blue binder is its reciprocity, its lesson: never discount these students or their motives or the rural worlds from which they have come.

When the university in farm country comes around to thinking about food, it has no idea, just a hunch, how much it will fill its pantry with beef, carrots, flour, berries—the work of neighbours.

Easter Weekend

Focus. Don't make the last person who walks in the door your highest priority. Manage time and access. Unless it is a student and her mother with serious things to say, an incriminating phone message to play.

Focus. Consult HR and legal. Trust your instincts. Call police. Get involved. What do we know for sure? What can we disclose? Can we suspend immediately? What help does the student need?

Deliver the letter by hand. No one home.

On Easter morning he takes the call, 3 A.M. Suspect in custody, warrants from elsewhere too, thanks for all the help.

He skips the resurrection, way too much adrenalin, enough to roll a stone away. He gives his daughter a lecture she didn't need on the perils she must avoid. He meets classes, mollifies students. He sends an email to the campus, what people need to know. Someone must have forwarded it to the newspaper, which might be calling. Never mind. What help does the student need now?

Two years later, her name is called. She crosses the stage, past the row of platform dignitaries. He has a diploma for her. *Thank you*, he says, just loud enough, *for your courage*. Though only she will know how much it took.

Years of Promises to See this Day

What students know is that for two weeks in September the doors of the new library have stayed closed—a clever ruse, having them demand to be let in. They know nothing of brinksmanship over dollars, deadlines and final inspections, or the logistics of shelving to Library-of-Congress perfection. Those stories have been tucked away for a celebration.

As the doors open, the most serious students, as if they wear blinders, stride past balloons and doughnuts towards the tables with the window views. They plant backpacks as markers, staking claims for a semester. At 9:02 or so, Garrett Thorson signs out the first book.

This library is for students, maybe the next two generations of them. But at the microphone all he can think to say is that if students should see tears in the eyes of their professors it is because some of them have endured twenty and thirty and, looking at Doc Larson, almost forty years of promises to see this day.

Round Dance

The tobacco on the table, the elder who was once his student accepts the invitation. That was months ago, before the geese had gone.

The smudge-fire lit, the elder says a blessing in Cree. The pipe is passed around the circle of men. The line forms for bison stew, biscuits, blueberries—enough for hundreds on a cold night in January. Some have come from up the street. The sweet burn of braided grass unfurls to the four corners of the gymnasium, whose Lutheran builders in 1964 did not imagine it used for round dances, any dances, but who might have known an honest prayer when they heard it, holy when they stood on it, words made flesh when they saw them.

The skins warmed by an outdoor fire, the drummers sound a heartbeat. Dancers form two and three rings, whatever it takes. Children run in and out. Older feet shuffle, hips pivot as they can.

The elders in place, blankets received, thanks given, past graduates step forward on the stage as their names are called: Cree, Metis, Inuit, faces and bodies solemn, tremulous, surprised by the weight of their eagle feathers and the memory of having once lived in two worlds at one time, released when the honour song returns the room to drumming and dancing. They had not expected such a return.

The midnight plates of bologna sandwiches emptied, most of them, dancers fading, drummers and singers line up for their cash. It is 2 A.M. The gymnasium is quickly cleaned, but some things will not be tucked away, put back the way they were before.

Dog Sled

On the east arm of Great Slave Lake, where the ski-plane filled with fuel, hay bales and boxes of meat skids to a stop, there is a cabin and, outside it, expectant sled dogs who take to late-morning harness with barking as polyphonic as an orchestra tuning for the first baton.

In the files of the university there is a workplace injury report, submitted within the requisite 72 hours. It describes an incident in which the dean was invited to drive the sled soon after the trail left the flatness of the lake for the stunted woods, forgot to use the footbrake, struck a tree on slanted ice, cartwheeled over the bucket into hard snow, shook it off, rejoined the sled, listened with unfailing interest as students relived their two-week Arctic experience, but felt the leg stiffen in purples and yellows as the pilot took a low, looping, scenic route, cliff-side, across the lake and back to Yellowknife.

Those Who Build Bridges

There are professors who talk about bridges, for professors are profligate with metaphors; they mix them; or they claim to see right through them.

It is a rare and practical professor who builds a bridge with his own hands. A real bridge: an iconic wooden bridge astride the ravine, built in the heat of a single summer with salvaged timbers and geometric precision and student volunteers. The bridge everyone remembers. By the time that its frailties are exposed by flash-floods and the futile grasping of screws for solid timber, it will have borne the weight of a generation of stories, of romance, bravado, sanctuary and routine. There will be no saving it.

Good builders, though, build more than they know, more enduring than the thing itself.

While Stephen Lewis Sleeps

Stephen Lewis is asleep in the passenger seat, slung between time zones and speeches. His driver rehearses the introduction he will need to make that night for someone so skilled with words as the United Nations special envoy.

Stephen Lewis is asleep. A gymnasium is prepared for a thousand people on a prairie winter night. Students and teachers who know a school in Johannesburg, and so a little about HIV/AIDS, board a bus in Wainwright for the ninety-minute ride to hear him speak. Generous people from Viking check the weather and their watches so as not to be late. Long tables fill with items for a silent auction. The students on campus who persisted in their invitation finish the last of the recycled toothbrush bracelets they will offer for sale. One of them, a Ugandan, polishes the words she will say on stage.

Stephen Lewis is asleep. He does not stir even when his driver throws his plans into reverse; for what needs an introduction is not the speaker, he decides, but a campus, a community, a whole rural swath of conservative Alberta that is not what it might seem from a distance.

When Stephen Lewis takes his place on stage, he will see for himself how passion has found its match.

Highway Time

One hour and fifteen minutes, maybe less, is the time it takes to drive to University Hall, unless there is someone outside his door with a problem that won't wait or the fleet car needs gas or there is a shine on the highway that looks like ice—best to slow down— or a train at the junction or a tow-truck and two cars collided past Hay Lakes or a semi-load of chickens spilled in crates or a moose or a double-wide caravan of machinery starting to move or a construction delay westbound on the freeway or red lights all the way up 111th Street or a steady line of pedestrians at the hospital crosswalk or, almost there, a parking lot filled with craft-sale shoppers so close to Christmas.

So he is always almost late.

A Life as Thin as Paper

With his gloved hands, rough, not velvet, caked with concrete,
he has cupped a hummingbird, a thousand beats a minute; he has
pulled it from the roof truss where it rested, dull brown, still and
flat, like a moth, unsure the way to daylight. He has swung the
smallest of birds into flight.

With his own hand, too, unprotected, he has held a life as thin as
paper, held it, and let it go.

Straw-Men and Politicians

The call comes from an unknown number while he waits to buy a sandwich. No intermediary. No small talk. *That article of yours in that magazine*, says the politician, who is reading from a faxed copy of the first page, *some of the boys are asking why someone in your position would write this kind of thing. Someone who ought to be more careful.*

That first paragraph, the dean explains, defensive, then regaining his nerve, was meant to set up a straw-man. Use a little humour. Maybe it didn't work. But still, he thought, the politician would like the point.

The caller backed off. He just called, he said, to have some fun. Hard to say for sure, like it's hard to explain a straw-man to a politician.

Six Years, No Accidents

You can trust me, she says, by way of introduction, *six years, no accidents—I am a good driver*. She is at least a cautious one. She stops the car far short of the white line at the first intersection. She is nudged onto the Guangzhou highway only by a bus driver's insistent horn. She slows at the first raindrops. Her eyes rock, back and forth, between the highway and the GPS unit on her lap, which, muted, speaks no advice when she exits onto a narrower road or, caution thrown temporarily to the wind, pulls out to pass a flatbed truck up a long hill, oncoming traffic already at the crest, or, undaunted, swings to the truck's right where the road is filled with the basketed bicycles of an older economy.

In my country, he says, with pathological calm, *we don't do that*.

In that instant they each know that he has made a command and not a cross-cultural observation. She accepts her place behind the truck. When they get to Guangzhou, streets and skylines new since yesterday, newer than the satellite map in her lap, it is only when the word Westin appears out of steel and glass that they have a navigation point to follow to their destination. Relief, it seems, needs no translation.

She turns for home: six years, still no accidents.

A Curator of Tears

He gathers tears from full-grown men, who trust him with their stories.

I do not know what would have become of me without that place, they say, words the same, voices thin: a corporate leader, a dentist disarmed by a chance encounter, an elementary school teacher in a northern city. They tell about second chances, good people, spartan surroundings.

One of them once came around with his roommate, four decades later. They would have been trouble. They wanted to see their old residence hall. Up on the third floor they remembered how they plugged a door with buckshot to celebrate the end of the year. *Hey look*, one shouted to the other, *that door's still here*. Sure enough: pockmarks under coats of paint. *Buggers! They told me they kept my deposit to replace the door.* In the good old days that forfeited deposit must have paid a salary instead.

The real wonder of the place, he thinks, is not that it should have outlasted a century of reasons to close it down. That much is owed to mere thrift, patchwork, sacrifice. No, the wonder, the inheritance not to squander, is found distilled from grown men's tears.

Another Year, and No Disaster

A lone gunman in the library. A freight train with chemical cars derailed in the valley. A bomb to free the lab animals. A welder's spark, and wind. A blizzard that blows for days. Worst case always wins. The movie-script imaginations of those who get paid to plan against catastrophe find their deadliest possibilities on a university campus. God forbid that they should ever happen here.

In the emergency operations room, though it is, of course, an exercise, in real time, three hours, real enough, his adrenalin rises to the occasion.

The dean's worst nightmare is not that students earn a diploma without learning a thing, without a critical affection for the world. It is that he will be the one in a hospital room or in front of the microphones, having to say, I'm sorry, we weren't ready. When students write their last exams and evacuate the campus he is secretly relieved. Another year, and no disaster.

Job Description

He does not know if the network server is bigger than a breadbox. He does not process expense claims or replace the printer cartridges. He does not know how the mail gets to his desk. He does not clear snow or coddle the boilers through months of winter. He does not feed 400 students and more, three times a day, or bake the buns that they will smuggle from the cafeteria in baggy pockets. He does not strip asbestos from old classrooms. He does not counsel distressed students late at night. He does not send out invitations for special events—he just shows up with scribbled words to say. He does not guide teenaged applicants in dial-up towns through the labyrinths of registration. He does not wash the towels after a game. He seldom takes the first, loudest burst of parent or public complaint. He does not help students change their major or check that they can graduate. Daily he is reminded of what he does not know, of the tangled workings of a small campus when it needs to fall into its seasonal routines, or remember, or change.

He does not try new ways to teach. He does not take students to other countries, their bags overpacked with fears and caricatures, hormones and wanderlust. He does not imagine a new curriculum. He makes no art or music. He scarcely remembers what it is, year after year, to find fresh energy for the classroom. He admires his colleagues who do all this. He is, at best, a part-time teacher and scholar—that much by force of will.

Sometimes he misses the rhythms, the satisfactions, of that world.

His job description is a string of gerunds, unfinished actions, with a face to fit each one: welcoming, translating, promoting,

   making friends, juggling, reconciling, conferring,

     sifting, filtering, hectoring, defusing,

        repeating himself,

thinking ahead, setting agendas, saying no, giving permission, heading off trouble, finding a way, keeping his lists. One thing, and then another. When he leaves for home in the dark he cannot say what he has accomplished, whether he has done it well or soon enough.

In a bookstore in Stockholm he laughs out loud at Stanley Fish, who is no longer a dean, but still takes down old leaflets, summons staff to clean up crumbs or a stack of discarded books in a hallway, still feels responsible for everything.

Truth be told, he is unsure that when the time comes he will know how not to be dean.

This Is the Way the World Will End or, How a Dean Thinks

Memorandum: As you are aware, there has been considerable speculation as to whether today, Saturday, May 21, would be the day on which a small number of the faithful are taken up in a great rapture. Needless to say, I am still here. While I will note that I have had no email communication to this point from anyone on campus, I have every reason to expect that all members of Executive Council will be in their offices on Tuesday following the holiday weekend. By university policy, department chairs have been determined not to be rapture-eligible.

If you should learn that staff members in your units have disappeared, please forward such information immediately to the Dean's Office so that it can inform budgetary reconsiderations around open positions.

AROUND 1

Someplace, Not No-Place

The prophets of disruption warn of change through innovation, though, such strange jeremiads, there is silver in the reckoning. Which must surely be at hand. For universities are like bookstores, they say, like bookstores used to be, quaint, unplugged, only less attuned to the desires of their customers, and someday soon the worldwide web will wash them out to sea—most of them—if they don't ride that wave instead, get out ahead of it. So hurry, digitize the greatest minds, tear down all the walls to learning, go global, balance budgets. All at once.

The prophets of disruption have not been to Wise, Virginia, which is someplace, not no-place, where the people of the half-spent coalfields send their children to the college, where face-to-face professors teach too much and earn too little, where the chancellor, a scientist, brought town and gown together in the name of Mister Jefferson and was laid to rest by thousands, eulogized by rival preachers, one of them a Baptist, and the sign on Main Street plainly said he would be missed.

Saturday Morning at the Co-op

He likes to start at the fruits and vegetables. His list is organized by the store's layout. He picks bananas, oranges, maybe apples, plums or BC peaches when in season, a pomegranate once or twice a year. He can only hope the romaine will be fine once his garden greens are done. In front of the bell peppers, the ones the Hutterites grow, he sees a friendly face from the concert last night. He enjoyed it, he says, *but it sure would be nice if you could get that parking lot fixed up. When's that going to happen?*

In dairy—milk, check; yogurt, check; cheese, check—a former student introduces her baby. She talks about a new business. She looks happier, he thinks.

There is no basmati in the next aisle. Again. Is it only in Camrose, only at the Co-op, or has it disappeared from shelves around the world?

Towards the coffee, he asks the woman he meets how her husband is doing after surgery. He makes a note to send a card.

The meat manager steps out from behind the counter. *Must soon be time for students to be back. Next week, is it? And I hear you've got another building going up. That's got to be good.* He invites the man to come to campus some time, see it for himself, as if he were dispensing sausage samples and two-for-one coupons.

In the aisle that segregates the foreign foods, mostly Dutch-Indonesian, Thai, curries, salsas and canned chilies, a student is restocking shelves. He can never remember his name—Ian, something like that. He knows he has one more year left on a business degree; he'd like to stay at the store, work his way into management. *How hard would it be*, Ian asks, *for my girlfriend to transfer here to finish up? Who should she talk to?* He gives a name and says to let him know if she has any trouble.

Over in baked goods, the last stop, he checks his list. Everything but the basmati is crossed off. A retired professor stops to tell him he will teach that math course after Christmas, in fact, has signed his contract.

At the checkout, the girl at the till, the quick one, still in high school, scans his groceries. She asks about nursing, maybe sciences, she's not sure. How would she get a scholarship, she wants to know. He scribbles another note on the back of his list.

In the parking lot, he helps the father of a recent English graduate pick up an elderly woman's groceries spilled onto the pavement. His daughter is headed out east to do her master's degree, he says, as proud as is decent. Her mother is a little worried, though, her being so far from home.

He sets his own bags in the back of his car: responsible, healthy choices. Good thing. You have to be careful what you buy at the Co-op. Word would get around.

Doctor Fowler

She has brokered no peace, discovered no cures, written nothing that should win a Nobel Prize. She had no degree to her name, in fact, until the afternoon she was dressed in ceremonial robes and hooded in front of the Class of 2008. She was born in a farmhouse, not far away, in 1920. She has lived in the same small city most of her adult life. Her nomination must have raised some eyebrows when it came; for surely it will bring the university no global lustre.

In the streets where she is known by name, though, where her first name is enough, she is the pre-eminent citizen, a woman ahead of her time, and never for herself alone. She is the champion of learning and public service. She is the voice of reason in the Tuesday paper—sometimes protective, sometimes bold, always clear.

At the podium, Doctor Fowler takes only a few well-timed minutes to earn her degree with words as artful and dignified as her long life. On this afternoon, the university has got it right.

Reading University

The driver stops the F-350 in the dusty parking lot so that, window down, engine idling rough, he can confess that he never really learned to read, that he works in the mines up north with young men who cannot read, that it will be different—here he hesitates, tears in his eyes—for his grandson. This is his first time on campus.

On the dean's arm is the scarlet robe he wore on the hottest day in July to present fidgety eight-year-olds with the diplomas that certify that reading levels have been raised and cafeteria lunches consumed.

He misses the girl in a hurry to show her mom *her university* and stake her educational ambitions in this place. As if, invited, it is not a stretch for people like her to decide this might be for them.

Boundaries

The ultrasound is fine, nothing unusual. He is free to go. He towels the gel from his neck, slips the tie back into place beneath his shirt collar, draws it tight. He takes two or three full-length strides towards the rest of his day before he is called back by name. The nurse motions for him to meet her behind a wall. Someplace quiet.

I was going to call you at your office, says the nurse, her name unfamiliar, *but I saw you had an appointment this week.*

Relief comes first. Whatever this is about, it is not medical.

I have a friend, he has a PHD, says the nurse. *He's thinking he'd like to teach in a university. I said he should apply here. What would he need to do?*

She does not know his field. Maybe philosophy. He does not trade in false hopes—budgets are tight, positions are filled—but there is no harm in a little encouragement. Times are tough for PHDs. He hands the nurse his card. He says to have the friend send a CV, maybe call for an appointment. That's the last he hears of it.

When he tells this story to professors of nursing, months later, they agree, aghast: *how unprofessional.* He does not judge so harshly. He has lived there long enough. If anything, he says in her defence, he was pleased she knew there was a university in town.

First Things, and How Wine Was Served on Campus

1.
Victor was a farmer, an independent thinker, a socialist, which was his word. It meant whatever he wanted it to mean. He was a leader in his community. He took his turn on the county council, the old telephone mutual. People counted on him to be stubborn about the things that mattered. So he stood up to the hazardous waste plant. He turned his farm organic, grew fruit, in that climate north of the river, started a winery, and didn't stop until he got the right to sell it. He did things first, that is, the hard way.

2.
It was years before in Vegreville they met. The room was jammed with farmers, one hundred and fifty of them, one professor, nine politicians flown in from Ottawa—three towns a day, three days, three provinces—promising each speaker five minutes to fix the farm crisis once they got finished fighting over the TV cameras, on or off, and before they got on the plane for someplace in the south. He and Victor sat side by side at the witness table. Victor, he could see, had a single piece of paper filled with pictures, circles and arrows, fair prices, people in the countryside living well—the wisdom of a lifetime, and not time enough to describe or explain it properly. No one asked to see it after.

3.
The world did not end, not even close, on the night when bottles were uncorked on campus, when wine was served with dinner,

decanted beneath the silent disapproval of those black-and-white pastors high on the wall.

Best to say it happened the first time because the right hand of authority had not known what dinner the left hand of creativity had planned until the advertising was on the streets. He would have put his foot down, too, like people said he should, first put a proper policy in place, a process, no jumping the gun, except he asked whose wine it was, and it was Victor's, and Elizabeth's, and she could come to dinner with her daughters, join his table, and he could give a welcome at the banquet that recalled the day in Vegreville, the one-page drawing, his unmistakable mark, and in public he could praise a farmer on a night for food and music.

Resource Curse

When the garden grows above an oil patch, the serpent can dispense with bait-and-switch. Knowledge was never much of a temptation anyways. *Hey, farm-boy, why not leave school now? Why start? What's it going to get you, a job flipping burgers? Look at your friends. Why not go straight to the money, maybe six-figures, which gets you a truck, a quad, a snowmobile?* The serpent does not mention what happens when the knees or shoulders go, when the payments and the pre-school kids and the time away from classrooms make it hard to ever finish that degree.

In a resource town the teacher surrenders one class, then a second, to the travelling dean. Career Studies. *You tell them to go to university. I can't. Take all the time you want.* The dean takes the measure of the class by the postures in the desks. He does his best. He does not demean the work of those who work the rigs, the pipeline, the logging trucks, the mill, not in front of their adolescent children. He retreats into a paradox, not insincere: such a well-educated province, so few young people in school, all those engineers, managers, professionals arrived from somewhere else. *Think of it this way*, he says: *if you want to work all your life for someone from Saskatchewan or Ontario even, yes, school is a waste of time.*

The dean is no match for the serpent in this town. When he leaves the room, eyes will roll, bodies will rearrange themselves, ninety minutes closer to freedom.

AROUND 2

On Sunday They Will Walk

There is no room for dying in the calendar, only death, and no stopping it when it comes.

The dog is thirteen, once the runt of a mongrel farm litter, suddenly blind, bumping into things, struggling even at short walks. The last was when he slipped home at noon. When he can finally leave Friday at the office, he finds the dog on the kitchen floor, unable to stand. The floor is smeared dry.

That evening they stay as close as cheeks and noses. Carried outside, alone for a moment, the dog wanders in a half-circle, tumbles into the last of the retreating April snow. Again they stay close. Breathing slows. Sleep comes.

When he wakes the clock is shining 5:15. The dog is standing, stumbling, falling. He turns on a light. In a fevered instant the dog rolls tight, uncoils hard against a wall.

He pins the thrashing legs and head, towels off foam, wipes his eyes.

She who is the dog's favourite is a province away. With a phone call she is on the road for home.

He feeds the dog small pieces of burger and cheese, head to one side; he offers his wetted fingers for drink. Together they wait. Hours pass. When she is through the door the dog's tail thumps the floor with a final vigour. The waiting is over.

She holds the dog's head in her lap. He says an ancient blessing: *The Lord make his face to shine upon you and give you peace.* It is no sacrilege.

He carries the dog to the back seat of the car—one more ride in a lifetime of rides. She sits beside.

The vet is gentle, the drug is efficient, the sun is setting towards late afternoon when they emerge.

On Sunday they will walk. On Monday the calendar will reclaim him.

Leave a Message at the Tone

What sign was it that when he said the blessing at the Christmas table, exhausted, the word on which he landed was not amen, so be it, but goodbye, as if he had just left a message for someone who was temporarily away from the phone.

What hope was it that God, endlessly busy, would get back to him?

The Under-Painting

She begins each canvas with swirls of strong colour that are meant to disappear beneath fresh layers of paint but give depth to the painting that emerges. Don't get attached to it, she used to say.

How quickly she is become something like an under-painting to the portrait of the public figure who is, for all to see, warm, wise, bold, successful. By the time it is done, she says, she will be invisible.

He is fond of under-paintings to the point of sadness, like he misses her when she goes to Barcelona, but in each case he knows the reason why. When this is over, he thinks, it will not help, not exactly, for anyone to thank her for her sacrifice.

A Wednesday Night in Daysland

He seldom lacks for company. He travels with his title and the job he needs to do. They fortify his confidence. When he walks into a room, he knows, his title will have made the introductions in advance. When his entry is unexpected, his title can cut short sentences, turn laughter awkward, force a premature hush. He is grown used to it.

How different on a Wednesday night in winter, on a concert night in Daysland, when the widened prairie Main Street is lined with trucks and cars, angle-parked, and the Palace is full, lights already out by the time that they arrive; when the two of them—just she and he, no title, no job to do—shed their coats against the same soft seats as always, I-6, I-7; when the emcee, his voice as reliable as single-malt, calls the singers to the stage, then takes his seat beside them, and asks beneath the tuning of the band how they are tonight. There will be an encore at the end, there always is, and friends to greet, and talk of music, trains and farming, maybe children; and until he checks for messages and they turn onto the highway he can be the man he thinks he is, or was.

Generation Gap

Someday, says his son, home from Lusaka and malaria and rickety bicycles on crowded streets and schools in squatter compounds with students who have no place next to go, home from Tehran and museums of torture and old men in villages and mosques in Qom, home from breakfast at Stella's on Sherbrook Street. *Someday*, he says, *I'd like a job as stressful as yours. Not yet.*

Brainstorm

It only happened once like this.

The storm that spun inside his head was like the juddering image cast by an old film projector, sprocket slipping, bulb burning, or the rotating-drum backdrop of a cheap cartoon, or the kind of febrile sleep in which a dream-scene replays for hours, so it seems, without plot or resolution; except that he was in a meeting, he had just spoken, and he could not remember what he said or, studying the faces in the room for clues, what sense he might have made.

It only happened once like this.

Return to Aberystwyth
For Elise on her 25th birthday

He peeled an orange at the top of the world, looking out over Cardigan Bay. Then section by section he ate it.

The sky was clear, the mood melancholic.

The last time and all the times before, they had come here as a family, packed a lunch, walked past the sheep and the farmhouse, climbed the earthen bank to eat. Then they left for home across the ocean. Time passed. Children made their own departures.

Orange eaten, peel scattered, the mood was melancholic, the sky was clear at the top of the world, enough to follow the coastline far to the south and north.

Not from that height, not on that day would he see how the arms do link up again in time.

Turning 50

The summer he turned 50 the last thing he wanted was a party. He could not say what else he wanted.

When friends came to the house with the gift of homemade jam, raspberry red, it was more than he expected and all that night he needed.

THROUGH

SE 09 31 06

1.
The grass stands tall from a rainy spring on the night he arrives at the land. The windshield is smeared with bugs. The headlights catch a young deer through the barbed-wire gate. The trail is marked just enough to follow in fading light. The trailer that had been jostled behind a big, borrowed F-350, weeks earlier, into a low spot, invisible from the road, is still in its place. The moon will soon lift, full of light, to diminish the mid-summer dark. The quiet is unnervingly antiquarian.

About that quiet: at 10:30 on the first morning, then again on the second, a single fighter jet flies directly overhead, low and loud, on a training exercise. No homesteader ever had such a bracing welcome here.

2.
The first days he works alone, no cellphone, no email, only a solar-powered radio and the voices of self-doubt for company. On the half-hour the radio cycles stories of storm warnings, court verdicts and summer festivals. In between, and after sundown, the voices of self-doubt have time to talk.

They bought this land two years earlier: off the grid, no beachfront, only sand, grown over with grasses and badger brush, some of it native prairie.

Why own it? The voices of self-doubt begin their interrogation: He who must trust his judgement every day is sure he has made a mistake. What ill-considered nostalgia, he thinks, what need of reconciliation or refuge or maybe rural credibility has brought him to this place, not so far from where he lived as a boy? He wonders whether he has become the kind of absentee landowner who pushes up land values while contributing nothing, not even a census tick, to the community. Before he bought he asked for reassurance on that precise point. But in the wettest summer in recent memory, all that grass stands ungrazed—in full public view.

I do not have the skills to do this, he writes in large letters.

He does not know enough to take on the responsibility: not enough about grasses, not enough about priming a pump and coaxing water from a shallow well, sand-packed at the tip, not enough about the brand-new generator from the Peavey Mart into which he rations gasoline.

3.
There is one more thing he thinks as he works, hidden beneath the horizon, turning a pile of stud-length 2x4s, deck boards and PVC panels into a respectable privy and solar shower. Though he cannot see a soul, the countryside, he knows, is no place for an introvert. He needs to meet the neighbours. Otherwise they'll be suspicious.

4.
The frog does not catch his eye until sometime after he has planted his foot alongside it. Camouflaged by the sandy, grown-over surface of the well that is sunk a cool, damp metre below ground-level, it

sits absolutely still. It does not move even when, he notices, a deer mouse begins to nibble at it. At the motion of his boot the mouse retreats into the sidewall, having made its point about the rough justice of nature and the limits of camouflage.

5.
When she arrives, as she had promised, he has shed all visual clues about his jacket-and-tie office identity. The salty sweat-lines on his cap confirm he has not been idle. After three days in hot sun and wind, most of his water has been consumed in large swallows. He is careful to keep his doubts to himself. This was, after all, his idea. And they have two weeks to go.

6.
They sleep differently here. They each dream, but in fragments, not in stories that can be recounted. They sleep well past 4 A.M. sunrise. Living outdoors is exhausting.

Constantly they watch the skies as clouds form and colours change, wonder and danger unfold in tandem. This is the temporary simplicity of their lives. Every afternoon thunderheads build, the radio reports warnings, an endless summer of rains, floods, tornadoes. Most days the storms pass to the north and south, parting at a well-placed bend in the river. The one that doesn't divide comes at them broadside with a fury: three hours of wind, rain and strobe-lightning. In the morning all is calm.

They are nowhere near a lake or an ocean, but when the wind blows the tall grass moves in waves. They wade in it. Only there is no shore, so no undertow.

7.
Once he has confessed his ambivalences, they take turns holding onto them. When visitors come, mostly family, bumping over a partly scythed track, unsure that this is the right place, they scrutinize their faces and voices for signs of bewilderment. They stumble when they are asked what they have planned. They do not talk about it when they are alone.

8.
At a family wedding for which he has cleaned up, a cousin says: *So, I hear you're going farming.* Well, not exactly, he replies.

9.
One evening they are walking with the dog down a gravel road—an unusual recreation in the countryside. A truck pulls slowly out of a farm driveway and passes them. They are the *new people*.

10.
The horizon line of a rural upbringing, he reads, signifies both escape and return. From the ridge at night he can see the clustered lights of his hometown in the distance and, in late afternoon, the sun-brightened hills beyond it where sky and land finally meet. There is more in that long view than he is able or unafraid to say.

11.
They wait every day for the young deer, a white-tail. Sometimes she watches from the ridge. One night she stands silhouetted along the north fence-line till the last blue in the sky deepens to black.

There are still meadowlarks here. Barn swallows, a squadron of three, circle overhead, once or twice in the afternoons, then turn back south. A brown female cowbird makes herself at home around the campsite. Cacti bud and blossom in soft yellow especially on the south-facing sides of hills. Bluebells and roses, pink and white, round out the palette.

Coyotes howl close at night. Pronghorn and elk, they've been told, migrate through this land, though not in mid-summer.

12.
At the hardware store the cashier asks for their phone number to ring in a small purchase. *We're not really from around here*, they say, but, having seen a news item about the arrest of a convicted criminal, living and working in town, hiding out from US justice, they assure her they are no fugitives. The cashier is startled, then relaxes. That criminal, she says, was a customer in the hardware. His name's still in the database. *You just never know*, she says, *even in a small town.*

13.
The schoolhouse like the post office was Wingello, district no. 2361, opened in 1910, closed during the Depression when there were neither children nor dollars enough to pay a teacher, then closed for good when children could ride the bus to town.

Surely the people is grass. In this landscape the homestead era has vanished almost without a trace, except for the cemeteries, which surely contain as many dead as there are still living. At the church across the fence-line, its weather-vaned steeple elegant on the horizon, immigrant Norwegians once insisted on oak flourishes; their daughters raised the money for a bell and a pump organ. They finished the church just in time to bury children dead of scarlet fever.

Though no word of God has been preached or sung inside for a long time, the spirit still blows through the cemetery, where it will.

To the north a Metis graveyard from the last days of the buffalo hunt rests quiet above the river. To the east, in the place where he spent Sunday mornings as a boy, where hymns of skies unfurled as scrolls made sense, the names on the headstones conjure a community of faces: stern, exuberant, gentle, stoic.

In a landscape such as this the ancient prophet will be heard: *All flesh is grass, and all its beauty is like the flower of the field. And then it fades. And its place knows it no more.*

14.
The map of a rural municipality is the gossipy archive of local geopolitics. It exposes secrets, alliances, the rise and fall of families. It passes no judgement.

The most recent edition has recorded their arrival, too, as plain as fact. The map does not say if they belong, if they will put the land to good use. It knows nothing of their desire or the shape their lives will take or the changes they will return, sun-worn, wind-burned, to face.

SET ON A WALL 2

Numbering the Days

The span of his working life, how far it reaches, how it will end, he cannot know.

His father though was only 54 when the tremors started, the slight shuffling, the doctoring, the dopamine. The loss of confidence.

By this rude measure he numbers his days: to take another term could be the last job that he does.

His mother, the keeper of calendars, tells him when she calls he should not work so hard.

The Old Man in Winter

1.

The frail old man in winter, in a picture, Chester Ronning, was the first he knew of Camrose and the place he'd come to teach.

Chester Ronning, born in China, far inland from foreign ports, learned his rhymes, his tones, his *hanzi*, wore the pigtail like the rest.

Chester Ronning, born in China, sailed past boxers, gunboats, hunger, heard young whispers of rebellion, borrowed clothes for Canada.

Chester Ronning wrangled horses, led a choir, ran a college, wrestled farmers in the Thirties for the money for a floor.

Chester Ronning got elected, speaking for the manifesto, a cooperative future—not a world of profiteers.

Chester Ronning, born in China, always leaving, under orders, left his mother in a graveyard, left the school his father founded, left the embassy in Nanking to the reds; but in the time of Nixon he took a trip back to his birthplace, to the grave, the school, in Fancheng, to the Great Hall of the People, where he wished that Zhou Enlai could come to Camrose for a meal.

Chester Ronning, born in China, never lost his native language, or the sense of feeling new in Canada with borrowed clothes.

2.

The frail old man in pinstripes, in a picture, Chester Ronning, was the one outside his office who would greet him every day. He packed the old man's story in his travels, in the halls of rural Alberta, in the countryside in Norway, and in China most of all. When he welcomed Chinese students, far from home, awash in English, he could not share a joke in Cantonese; but he learned to say, to their surprise, and his as well, that this of all the schools in Canada they might have picked was built by those first formed in China.

His last days in the office he unfurled a relayed message. DAD, it said, in upper case, would have been proud and grateful for his work. Kind things. The note is one to keep, of course, not because he counted himself in the same company, only a steward of the same small field.

In those last days, too, he took a break to greet a man come all the way from Chongqing to see the home of Chester Ronning. And they stood beside the picture for a picture.

Iron Cage

When it was that he crossed over, he does not remember, only that there is no way back, only, dimly, that there was a time when he was pleased with his primitive technology, when it seemed remarkable, even ridiculous, that another dean should answer emails on his phone in a grocery aisle on weekends or an airport in Europe or minutes before his wedding, or when the rituals of early morning did not begin with the inbox of a handheld screen: a request from the Provost, awake already, or the *Chronicle*'s dispatches from the world of higher education.

Now virtue and necessity conjoin in microchips. He is never out of reach. He can keep up with his job. He can read and answer 200 messages a day; professors, students, department chairs, editors expect that he will. He is relieved of the temptation, surely a selfish one, to concentrate on just one thing, alone, for a long time.

Someday he will sit down in a quiet place to reread Max Weber: offices and machines, efficient rationality, discipline turned to moral duty. The book he thinks is in a box in storage. Next time he checks his email he can Google iron cage.

The Image of a Hundred Years

The cookies on the plate are the marshmallow kind, factory-made half-globes with chocolate skins, a graham crumb base, red faux-fruit inside. The kind you won't find in well-catered enclaves. The plate is set with a cup of tea, beside the recliner-rocker in which he has been directed to sit, once his friend Elsie, Class of '33 or so, has made the introductions. The plate is meant for him alone. But it comes with expectations to eat the cookies and listen and look at photographs, which he does, until he fastens on the one in sepia: two young women on the prospect that is his campus. There is no mistaking it. One of the women, he is told, was a teacher at the college, a relative who came north from Minnesota for only a couple of years. Maybe 1916. Maybe earlier. From where the women stand, unposed, all things still are possible.

He asks to take the photograph with him. Big as a poster, it will be the image of a hundred years.

Reminders

He reminds himself and sometimes says that once he was a young turk too, with things to change and wrongs to right for others' sake, a career to make without a guide, or so it seemed, though his impatience was soon tempered by the desire of his students and the dreams he dreamed with colleagues and the care the elders showed him for the place that they had made.

He reminds himself, and does not say, not often enough, that it is no small thing for a professor after twenty years or thirty to summon all the fearlessness to teach again in fall—and good for those who do.

He reminds himself and says, just once, that when his brow is furrowed it just might signal more intensity than he intends.

He reminds himself but does not say, does not think till later to put it clear as this, that it is better to empty out than hollow out, and good to know the difference; for he could be all things to all people, he could fix every problem and find the right words for every occasion and answer all his emails before midnight, and still he could be hollowed out a little at a time.

But empty, empty can be filled again.

Last Night in June

The rituals of leave-taking, in the end, were as simple and practised as those at any Holiday Inn: scan the room one last time, leave the keys on the desk, pull the door shut, locked, behind him.

The time for words had passed. Mercifully so. He had left his faculty without a fight, only an apology for the things he got wrong in eight years of words, decisions, actions. He had stood at a last farewell, cake untouched, and said that he now understood his great-grandfather, a settler in Oklahoma, telling his neighbours, no, he would not reverse his decision to go to Canada, not after such a struggle to make it, but offering reassurance too: for he knew he would be a stranger the rest of his life.

On that last long night in June he was alone in the building. The sun lit the office in bronze, enough so that he could shake crumbs from the desk drawers and straighten the digital files. He gathered his music, his pictures, the Expos coffee mug he had carried from Olympic Stadium in 1989, a Mother's Day promotion, an afternoon when Dennis Martínez beat the Giants 4–3.

His first trip to the parking lot, the mug fell from the box. He put the pieces in the bin. This was not a night for signs or sentiment. The Expos had left Montreal long ago.

His last trip, when he could only go out, not back in, he took the long staircase, pausing when he reached each level, as if awaiting some clear insight or storm-cloud of emotion. He could only think how much of himself he would leave behind and how strange that, come tomorrow, he should have an invitation to return.

Notes

Preface

For more developed fragments of memoir and reflections on higher education and place, see my *We Are All Treaty People: Prairie Essays* (Edmonton: University of Alberta Press, 2008), including the final essay, "A University at Home in the Rural"; and the introduction written with my co-editor Bill Spellman in *Roads Taken: The Professorial Life, Scholarship in Place, and the Public Good* (Kirksville, MO: Truman State University Press, 2014).

Hard Times

This piece paints something of the atmosphere of prolonged crisis and quiet desperation that prevailed at what was then Augustana University College, which had built an enrolment of about a thousand students, many of them from rural and northern communities, and a reputation for undergraduate education in the liberal arts, but which had never achieved a secure financial footing. By the 2002–3 academic year, it had reached a precarious state. In that year, Augustana experienced heightened faculty–administration tensions, the threat of mass layoffs, the departures of good colleagues, and, in spring, the emergence of the surprise option of incorporation into the University of Alberta—a rare and complex case, these days, of a private post-secondary institution being brought into the public university system. That option required a national denominational-church body to relinquish formal ownership, the Government of Alberta to commit funding for operations, capital improvements, and debt retirement, and the University to absorb employees and degree programs. By a series of small miracles, all this happened just in time for a formal ownership transfer on July 1, 2004. My own early involvement in supporting the University of Alberta option led to an appointment as interim dean and vice-president (academic) in advance of formal negotiations. Others, of course, made their own important contributions and will have their own memories of that time.

Vikingskipshuset, Oslo

The *Vikingskipshuset* or Viking Ship Museum in western Oslo contains three ancient boats unearthed in the late 19th and early 20th centuries from burial mounds in farmers' fields. One of them, the Oseberg, was excavated with its grave goods, disassembled, and dried out over two decades in an Oslo warehouse before it was reassembled—almost entirely with original timbers—and moved in 1926 by railcar on temporary track through central Oslo before being floated across the fjord to the museum built for it. See http://www.khm.uio.no/english/visit-us/viking-ship-museum/exhibitions/oseberg/.

Reciprocity

On May 15, 2003, a single cow with bovine spongiform encephalitis (BSE) was discovered on a farm in northern Alberta. The US border, like other international markets, was immediately closed to Canadian beef; and small cow-calf producers, operating at the most vulnerable end of a highly concentrated, highly integrated North American industry of massive feedlots and packing-plants, bore the greatest economic impact. Over the next decade, the combined effect of BSE, drought, and rising feed costs was a sharp drop in the number of both beef producers and cattle in the province.

Years of Promises to See this Day

When a spectacular new library was opened in 2009, the first new building on campus in two decades, long-time staff members told stories of promises made when they were hired, of architectural drawings, sites roped off, signs posted, so that some were determined not to believe it was real until construction was well advanced. Garrett Thorsen really was the first student to sign out a book.

Those Who Build Bridges

When a new land crossing across a campus ravine replaced an iconic wooden bridge that lasted three decades before spring flooding exposed its rotting timbers, it was time to honour Dr. Orlando Olson, physics professor and engineer, under whose direction the old structure had been built by late-summer volunteers, and to tell stories of the things that had happened on, off, and under that bridge.

While Stephen Lewis Sleeps

Stephen Lewis was the UN Secretary-General's special envoy for HIV/AIDS in Africa when he spoke at the Augustana Campus on the invitation of students.

Highway Time
Highway 21 is the most direct route between Camrose and Edmonton, where the University's other campuses and administrative offices are located.

Job Description
The book to which I refer is *Save the World on Your Own Time* (Oxford: Oxford University Press, 2008) by Stanley Fish.

This Is the Way the World Will End or, How a Dean Thinks
Harold Camping, the American radio preacher, famously prophesied that the Rapture and Day of Judgement would occur on May 21, 2011. He later recanted his prophecy. I trust that the real memo on which this meditation is based will be discovered in the files decades from now.

Someplace, Not No-Place
At the time of his death, David Prior was chancellor of the University of Virginia's College at Wise. He was both a mentor and a colleague with whom I served on the executive committee of the Council of Public Liberal Arts Colleges. See also my tribute first published as "Real Impact," *Inside Higher Education*, posted February 27, 2012, at http://www.insidehighered.com/views/2012/02/27/essay-how-chancellor-can-change-community.

Doctor Fowler
Berdie Fowler (1920–2013) received the first honorary Doctor of Laws degree conferred by the University of Alberta at a convocation at Augustana Campus. This piece draws partly on my words in nominating and then introducing her on that occasion.

First Things, And How Wine Was Served on Campus
Victor Chrapko (1942–2008) farmed with his wife Elizabeth near the town of Two Hills. He and I were the first two presenters to the House of Commons Standing Committee on Agriculture and Agri-Food in Vegreville, Alberta, on December 9, 1999. My comments were revised as "'Farm crisis' not just a matter of net income," *Edmonton Journal*, December 17, 1999; and reprinted in "What is the Farm Crisis?

Seven Short Commentaries," *We Are All Treaty People: Prairie Essays* (Edmonton: University of Alberta Press, 2008), pp. 146–48.

SE 09 31 06

The title of this piece refers to a rural land description in a form that is familiar to prairie people, who could find it on a map if I added "west of the third meridian."

The texts in section 13—"Surely the people is grass"; "All flesh is grass, and all its beauty…"; "the wind passes over it…and its place knows it no more"—are drawn from the Book of Isaiah 40: 6–8 and from Psalms 103: 15–16 (Revised Standard Version).

The Old Man in Winter

Chester Ronning returned from teaching in China to serve as principal of the former Camrose Lutheran College from 1927 to 1942, during which time he was elected once to the provincial legislature and briefly held the position of leader of the new Co-Operative Commonwealth Federation. Immediately after World War II, he began a distinguished diplomatic career that included postings in China, Norway, and India, as well as an unsuccessful special mission to Hanoi to mediate an end to the Vietnam War that famously angered President Lyndon Johnson when Ronning criticized the US bombing campaign as unhelpful to peace. He remained a public critic of the war. Ronning died at his home in Camrose in 1984, having returned to China in later life at the invitation of Premier Zhou Enlai, who received him in the Great Hall of the People. For further background see Brian Evans's biography, *The Remarkable Chester Ronning: Proud Son of China* (Edmonton: University of Alberta Press, 2013), and Tom Radford's wonderful documentary, "China Mission: The Chester Ronning Story" (1980), which can be viewed on the National Film Board of Canada's website. The photograph to which I refer is found in Tom Radford, ed., *Alberta, A Celebration* (Edmonton: Hurtig, 1979), p. 87. I told my own Ronning story at the start of the essay "'Their Own Emancipators': The Agrarian Movement in Alberta," in *We Are All Treaty People: Prairie Essays* (Edmonton: University of Alberta Press, 2008), pp. 59–60.

Acknowledgements

I CONTINUE TO BE GRATEFUL to many people, first of all at the Augustana Campus, throughout the University of Alberta, and in Camrose and east-central Alberta, for the trust I was given to do an extraordinary job in extraordinary times. For sake of brevity and for fear of omission, I will refrain here from naming individuals in each of those spheres, but hope that this book will provide new opportunities to thank people personally.

These meditations were begun in the southern Appalachians while I was on a subsequent leave at the University of North Carolina, Asheville, thanks to the invitation of Bill Spellman at the Council of Public Liberal Arts Colleges. There I was introduced to the poet Holly Iglesias in the office next door and, through her, to the genre of prose poetry. Holly graciously read the first small sample of my writing. Since then, Randy Kohan and Naomi McIlwraith have provided both affirmation and the shining example of their first books of poetry. My colleagues Olive Yonge, Heather Zwicker, Ellen Bielawski, and Brian Maraj—writers, scholars, and university administrators—read what I sent them and provided some of the encouragement I needed to see it into print. Lesley Cormack invited me to participate in a panel, "Life After Deaning," at the annual meeting of the Canadian Council of Deans of Arts, Humanities and Social Sciences, where some of these meditations were read aloud for the first time to an unsuspecting audience. Finally, I am grateful to the four anonymous reviewers for their thoughtful reading of the full manuscript from various places within the world of higher education—and for expressing so well in their own words what I had set out to do.

This is my third book with the University of Alberta Press. I'm mindful that each one has spilled across the catalogue categories by which academic publishers like to organize titles, and am most appreciative of the willingness to consider and help shape this unconventional artifact, whose completion was interrupted by a relapse into administration. I'm impressed again by the high standard of care that my colleagues in Ring House 2 show at every stage for books and for authors. Thanks Linda, Cathie, Peter, Alan, Mary Lou, Monika, Duncan, Basia, and Colleen. Thanks too to Maya Fowler-Sutherland for her careful editorial work with the text.

When I reread this manuscript, I am almost overwhelmed by the reminders that my greatest debts are those owed to members of my immediate family. In their own ways they absorbed the intensity and uncertainty of the hard times described in the meditation of the same name, and then, in the relative stability of the new institutional normal that followed, they paid the unaccounted price of a father and husband fully and publicly immersed in the dean's role—the way I knew to perform it. This artifact is for them too: for Stefan and Elise, who grew into fine adulthood in these years and have taken their own creative risks with words in print, with music and visual design; for Laurel and now Mateus, who have enlarged our family circle so wonderfully; and for Rhonda, who could not have known all she signed up for in 1980 but without whom I could not imagine either the years that have passed or those still to come. She is my first and most important reader. While her images in this book are small studies that aren't necessarily typical of her paintings, their strength, vivid colours, and attentiveness reflect the person I know her to be. It's a matter of deep pleasure for me to have my words appear next to them.

Also from The University of Alberta Press

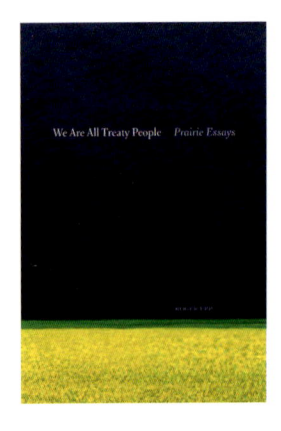

We Are All Treaty People
Prairie Essays
ROGER EPP

Provocative essays explore the poetry and political economy of life in Canada's rural West.

More information at www.uap.ualberta.ca